Better Homes and Gardens®

OUTER SPACE

Hi! My name is Max. I have some great projects to show you – and they're all about space! We're going to have lots of fun making them together.

Inside You'll Find...

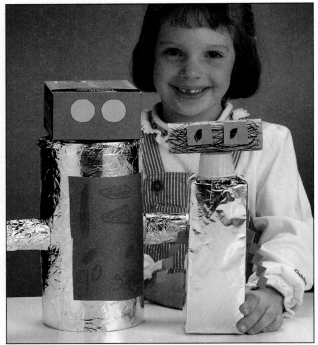

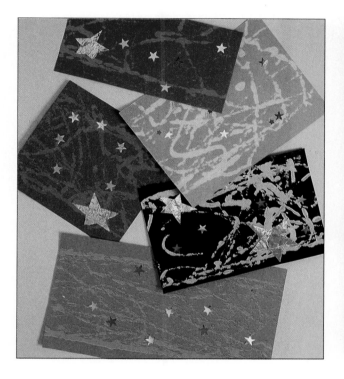

Get to know the planet Mars and search for hidden objects.

Space Explorers

Max and Elliot are exploring the planet Mars for rocks. Hidden in the picture are 10 things that they probably wouldn't find on Mars. Can you find them?
The answers are on page 30.

Did you know...

● Mars is known as the red planet because everything on it is a reddish color.

● The surface of Mars is like a desert with volcanos and canyons.

● So far, no one has found any life on Mars. But Mars is like Earth in other ways. It has seasons like Earth does, but they last longer than ours. And, a day on Mars lasts about the same time as a day on Earth—24 hours.

● It is much colder on Mars than it is on Earth. That's because Mars is much farther away from the sun than the planet Earth is.

● Someday astronauts may travel to Mars, just as they traveled to the moon. Would you like to visit the planet Mars?

Change a cardboard tube into a vehicle for space travel.

Roaring Rocket

You can pretend to be an astronaut and fly your rocket into space. Ready?
Let's go. Five, four, three, two, one . . . Blast off!

What you'll need...

- Thin strips of crepe paper or ribbon, or 2 cotton balls
- Scissors
- Tape

- One 11- or 4½-inch cardboard tube (paper towel or toilet paper tube)
- Construction paper

- White crafts glue
- 1 small plastic or paper drinking cup

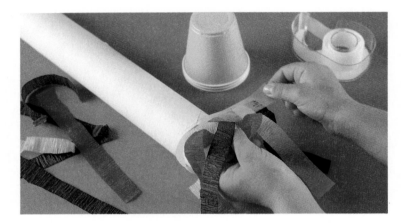

1 For the rocket fire, place several strips of crepe paper side by side so they touch. Cut a piece of tape that's longer than the width of all the crepe paper strips. Lay the tape across the top of the strips. Stick the tape with the crepe paper to one end of the paper towel tube (see photo). *Or,* tape the cotton balls to the tube.

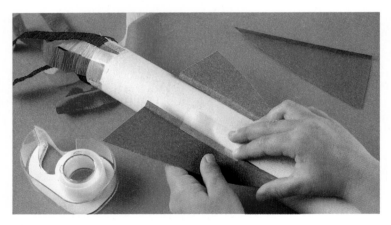

2 Cut 2 rectangles out of the construction paper. Cut 1 rectangle in half diagonally to make 2 triangles. Repeat with the other rectangle.

Make a narrow fold on the long, straight side of 1 triangle. Tape the triangle onto the rocket (see photo). Repeat with 2 or 3 of the remaining triangles.

3 For the capsule, glue the cup to the top of the rocket (see photo). Let dry. *Or,* cut a 4-inch circle out of construction paper. Then cut a pie-shaped wedge out of the circle (cut out about ¼ of the circle). Bring the cut ends together and overlap slightly to make a cone shape. Tape the ends together. Glue to the top of the rocket.

Combine imagination and a cereal box for an exciting space adventure.

Jet Pack

Make believe you're on a space adventure. Don't forget to wear your Jet Pack when you leave your rocket. It will move you around in space while you explore fun new places.

What you'll need...

- Scissors
- Construction paper
- 1 large cereal box
- Crayons or markers

- Tape or white crafts glue
- 1¼ yards of ribbon or heavy string

- 2 or 3 small plastic or paper cups or nut cups

1 Cut a piece of construction paper the same size as the front of the cereal box. Use crayons to draw the control panel for the Jet Pack on the paper (see photo). Tape the paper to the front of the cereal box.

2 With adult help, cut a slit in the middle of each side of the box near one edge. Push one end of the ribbon through a slit. Put your hand in the box. Pull the end of the ribbon through the box and push it through the slit on the other side (see photo). Pull the ribbon through the box until it's even on both sides.

3 Tape the ends of the cereal box closed. For rocket boosters, tape 2 or 3 cups to the bottom of the box (see photo).

Wear the Jet Pack on your back with the ribbon tied around your chest.

Your astronauts will be delighted to munch on these frozen treats.

Planet Pops

You won't have to go far to discover one of these creamy, cool planets. Just land in your kitchen and explore the freezer.

What you'll need...

- 8-cup glass measure or large bowl
- Two 12-ounce cans lemon-lime carbonated beverage
- One 14-ounce can sweetened condensed milk
- ¼ cup lemon juice
- Food coloring
- Foil
- Eighteen 3-ounce paper cups
- Table knife
- 18 wooden sticks

1 In the 8-cup measure, put the carbonated beverage, sweetened condensed milk, lemon juice, and several drops of food coloring (any color). Stir with a rubber scraper or spoon to mix (see photo).

2 Cut or tear eighteen 4-inch squares of foil.
　　With adult help, pour some of the carbonated beverage mixture into a paper cup. Press 1 square of foil over the top of the cup (see photo). Repeat with the remaining mixture, cups, and foil.

3 With the tip of the table knife make a small hole in the center of 1 piece of foil. Push a wooden stick into the cup through the hole (see photo).
　　Repeat with the remaining cups and wooden sticks. Freeze 4 to 6 hours or till firm.
　　To serve, remove foil and tear off the paper cup. Makes 18.

Big and Small Planets

Planets are many different sizes. You can make Planet Pops different sizes, too.

For bigger Planet Pops, use 5-ounce paper cups instead of the 3-ounce size. You'll need 10 cups and 10 wooden sticks.

Learn to recognize shapes and differentiate between sizes.

Space Station

Max is sitting at the controls of a space station. Look at all the buttons and dials. Can you point to the orange triangles, circles, squares, and ovals? How many of each can you count?

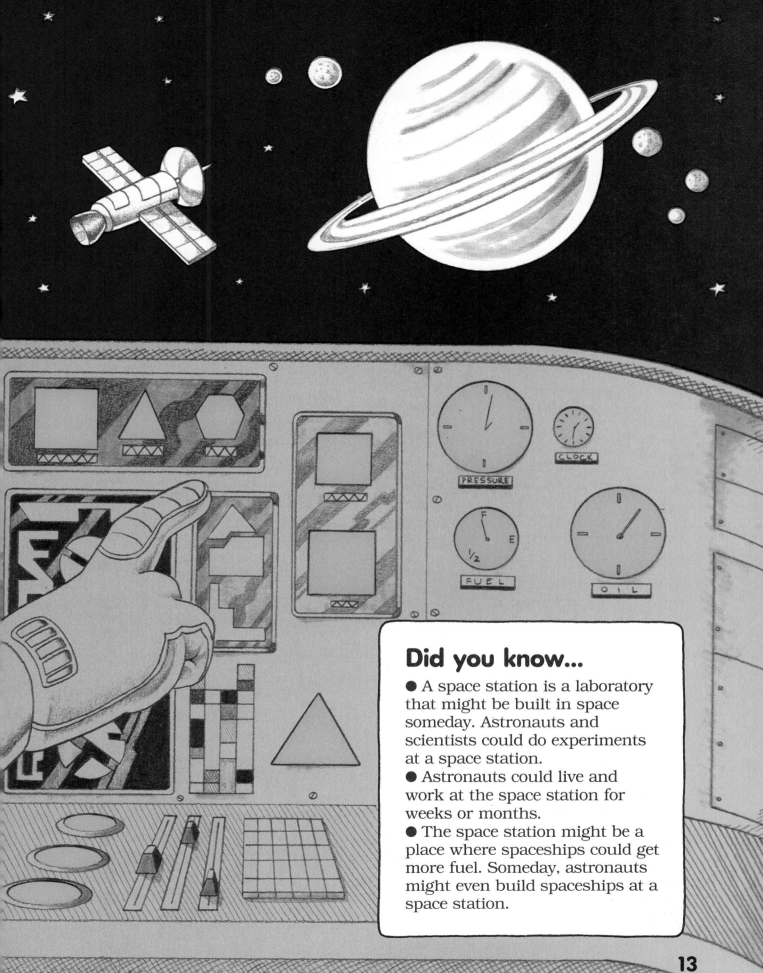

Did you know...

● A space station is a laboratory that might be built in space someday. Astronauts and scientists could do experiments at a space station.

● Astronauts could live and work at the space station for weeks or months.

● The space station might be a place where spaceships could get more fuel. Someday, astronauts might even build spaceships at a space station.

Command a space station from a shoe-box panel.

Control Panel

Pretend you're a space pilot. Push a button or turn a dial to launch a rocket.
What else can your Control Panel do?

What you'll need...

- Paper
- Crayons or markers
- White crafts glue
- 1 shoe box with lid
- Cotton balls or buttons
- 1 long twist-tie, folded in half
- Spool of thread
- One 11-inch cardboard tube (paper towel tube)
- Tape
- 1 pipe cleaner or drinking straw
- Plastic lid, egg carton cup, or nut cup
- Paper fastener

14

1 Sky Screen: Cut a square out of paper. Draw a picture of outer space on the paper with crayons. Glue onto box.

2 Orbit Switches: Glue cotton balls onto the box. Or, draw numbers or shapes on small squares of paper. Glue onto the box.

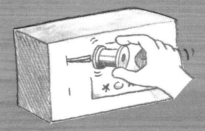

3 Lunar Tuner: Punch a small hole in the box. Push the unfolded ends of twist-tie through the hole about ½ inch. Bend ends flat against inside of box. Push the spool over the folded end of the twist-tie. Bend the folded end of the twist-tie over the edge of the spool.

 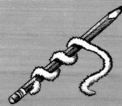 

4 **Steer Stick:** On the side of the box, trace around the end of the cardboard tube. With adult help, cut out the traced circle. Push the tube through the hole. If necessary, tape the tube to the inside of the box to secure it.

5 **Asteroid Antenna:** Wrap a pipe cleaner tightly around a pencil. Remove from the pencil. Gently pull on both ends of the pipe cleaner to separate the coils. Punch a hole in the shoe box with a pencil. Push the pipe cleaner into the hole.

6 **Gravity Disk:** Poke a hole in a plastic lid or egg carton cup. Then poke a hole in the box. Push a paper fastener into the plastic lid, then into the hole in the box. Bend the paper fastener prongs so they lie flat.

Design a futuristic-looking playmate with boxes and foil.

Shiny Robot

A robot is a machine that can do work without a person running it all the time. What kind of work does your robot do?

What you'll need...

- One 1-quart milk carton
- Tape
- One 14-inch-long piece of foil
- 1 nut cup or paper cup
- One 4½-inch cardboard tube (toilet paper tube)
- Markers or crayons
- Scissors
- Construction paper

1 Close the milk carton and push the top to one side so it's flat. Tape it down. For the robot body, lay the milk carton on its side near one end of the foil. Tape the edge of the foil to the side of the milk carton (see photo). Wrap the foil around the sides and ends of the milk carton. Use tape to hold the foil in place.

2 For the neck, tape the nut cup to the top of the body.
   For the head, color the cardboard tube with markers. Cut eyes out of construction paper. Tape them onto the cardboard tube. Tape the head to the neck (see photo).

3 For arms, cut 2 strips of construction paper each about 2 inches wide and 6 inches long. Fold the strips back and forth like an accordion (see photo). Tape the arms to the side of the body.
   If you like, use construction paper and crayons to make a control panel. Tape it to the front of the body.

Stars, Stars, Stars

Inspect the star patterns for hidden letters.

Max and his friend Ozzy are looking for groups of stars that make shapes. Tonight they've found some stars that look like letters. Do you see the letters S, T, A, and R hidden in the sky?

18

Did you know...

● Stars look very small because they are very, very far away from Earth. The stars are actually huge hot balls of gas.

● Our sun is a star. It is much closer to Earth than the stars we see at night. The sun gives us just the right amount of light and heat we need to live on Earth.

● Groups of stars that look like shapes are called constellations (kon ste LAY shuns). A long time ago, people gave names to these shapes made of stars. The Big Dipper and the Little Dipper are two constellations you can see in the night sky.

● Shooting stars aren't really stars at all. They're meteors (MEE dee ors). A meteor is a piece of a rock from outer space that burns up as it flies very fast through space.

A paint-covered ball creates the trail of a falling star.

Shooting Stars

Max thinks this kind of painting is fun because you don't know what the picture will look like until it's done. Try it and see.

What you'll need...

- Scissors
- Construction paper
- 1 large clean can or container with lid
- Tempera paint
- 1 small disposable container
- 1 table tennis ball or marble
- 1 disposable spoon
- Newspaper or brown kraft paper
- Foil and/or star-shaped stickers
- White crafts glue

1 Cut a piece of construction paper to fit inside the can. Put the paper inside the can so it stands up along the side (see photo).

Pour a little paint into the small container.

2 Put the table tennis ball into the paint. Use the spoon to roll it around until it is covered with paint (see photo). Use the spoon to put the ball in the can. Put the lid tightly on the can.

3 Shake the can several times or roll it around on a table or the floor. Take the lid off the can. Carefully take the paper out of the can and lay it on newspaper. Let it dry completely.

Cut stars out of foil. Glue them onto the paper. If you like, put star-shaped stickers on the paper, too.

Stars and planets orbit through a corn-syrup sky.

Jar of Stars

Have you ever made a wish on a falling star? Shake up your Jar of Stars and you can make lots of wishes while the stars slowly fall to the bottom. Then shake it again and make more wishes!

What you'll need...

- Light corn syrup
- 1 small clear glass jar with lid
- Water
- Food coloring
- Spoon
- Star Dust (see tip on page 23)
- White crafts glue
- Masking tape (optional)

1 Pour corn syrup into the jar until it's about ¾ full. Then fill the jar almost to the top with water. Add 1 or 2 drops of food coloring. Use a spoon to gently stir everything together (see photo).

2 Sprinkle a little Star Dust into the jar (see photo). If you like, stir the Star Dust into the corn syrup mixture.

3 Put some glue around the inside edges of the lid (see photo).
   With adult help, tightly screw the lid onto the jar. If desired, wrap a piece of masking tape around the side of the lid and the neck of the jar.

Star Dust

Sprinkle just one kind of Star Dust into your jar or mix them up. Try star-shaped sequins or shiny confetti, or glitter.

Or, tear a small piece of foil into tiny pieces. If you like, add circle-shaped sequins or shiny confetti to the jar for planets.

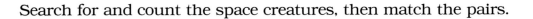

Search for and count the space creatures, then match the pairs.

Space Creatures' Spaceships

Oh my gosh! A flying saucer has landed on Earth and the Spacelings have gone exploring. Can you help Max and Elliot find the 10 Spacelings? Point to the Spacelings that look alike.

Did you know...

● Earth is the planet where we live. It is the only planet we know about that has life on it.
● Over half of Earth is covered by water. The rest of Earth is land.
● The part around the middle of Earth is called the equator. The temperature at the equator is very warm.
● The temperature at the top and bottom parts of Earth, the poles, is very cold.

A paper-plate spacecraft that really flies.

Flying Saucer

Max and Elliot are having fun playing outside with the Flying Saucer they made. While they play, they make up stories about who's riding in their saucer. What kind of story will you tell?

What you'll need...

- 1 heavy paper plate
- White crafts glue
- 1 paper bowl
- Markers or crayons

- Buttons, beads, ribbon, glitter, or stickers (optional)

1 Turn the paper plate upside down. Put glue around the top edge of the bowl (see photo). Turn the bowl upside down and press it onto the bottom of the paper plate. Let it dry completely.

2 To decorate the saucer, you can color it with markers (see photo). If you like, glue on buttons or other decorations. Let it dry completely.

Take your Flying Saucer outside and practice flying it.

A creamy hot filling comes wrapped inside saucer-shaped bread.

Spaceship Sandwiches

Max likes to have these sandwiches for lunch. They're yummy. While he's eating, he pretends he's the captain of a spaceship.

What you'll need...

- Shortening
- 1 baking sheet
- Filling Ingredients (see page 32)
- 1 mixing bowl
- Wooden spoon
- Table knife
- ½ of a 1-pound loaf frozen whole wheat bread dough, thawed
- All-purpose flour
- Rolling pin (optional)
- Pastry brush
- Milk
- Fork

1 Grease the baking sheet. Set it aside. Put the Filling Ingredients in a mixing bowl. Stir with a wooden spoon to mix well (see photo). Set aside.

2 Use a table knife to cut the bread dough into 8 pieces. With adult help, on a lightly floured surface roll or pat each piece into a 4- to 5-inch circle. Let the dough rest as needed.

   Place about *⅓ cup* of the filling onto 1 circle of dough (see photo). Repeat with remaining filling and 3 more circles of dough.

3 Brush milk on the edges of circles with filling. Place remaining circles on top, stretching to fit bottom circles. Press the edges together with the tines of a fork (see photo).

   Place on the greased baking sheet. Prick tops and brush with milk. With adult help, bake in a 375° oven 15 to 20 minutes or till golden. Cool. Makes 4.

Tasty New Territory

Explore new flavors inside your sandwich. Instead of beef, try other meats such as cooked pork or chicken. Or, use some leftover cooked vegetables instead of the carrot. Also, one 10-ounce package of refrigerated bread dough will work in place of the frozen bread dough.

Space Explorer

See pages 4 and 5

Here's the list of the 10 items hidden in the picture on pages 4 and 5: tricycle, telephone, football, cowboy hat, umbrella, picnic basket, chair, iron, skateboard, and bed.

● Reading suggestion: *Regards to the Man in the Moon* by Ezra Jack Keats

Roaring Rocket

See pages 6 and 7

Your children might enjoy learning how real rockets are launched into space by trying this fun science experiment.

● For the rocket, you'll need a bottle with a tight-fitting cork. (The cork is really the rocket.) Pour ½ cup *water* and ½ cup *vinegar* into the bottle. Wrap 1 teaspoon *baking soda* in a 4-inch square of a paper towel, twisting the ends to keep the soda inside. Take your experiment outside.

● Drop the paper towel with baking soda into the bottle. Push the cork in tightly. After the bottle is corked, tilt it on its side away from the people watching. It may take a few minutes for the rocket launch.

● This is what's happening. The vinegar penetrates the paper towel and reacts with the baking soda. Carbon dioxide gas is formed, building up pressure inside the bottle. Finally, the pressure forces the cork out of the bottle and the rocket flies upward.

Jet Pack

See pages 8 and 9

While your children play in their pretend space suits, tell them about what real astronauts wear in space.

● Temperatures in space range from very, very hot (from the sun) to very, very cold. The astronauts' space suits must be able to protect them from these extreme temperatures.

● The first layer they wear looks like long underwear and has a built-in cooling system. They call this a "spaghetti suit" because of all the tubes that are in it. The cooling system keeps the astronauts from getting too hot from the heat their bodies give off.

● The outer part of the space suit is 2 pieces. The lower section has the boots attached to the pants. The upper section around the chest and back is like a hard shell that doesn't bend. The pants and the arms are made of material that bends easily so the astronauts can move around.

● The upper and lower sections are held together with a belt around the waist. Astronauts also wear gloves and a helmet.

Planet Pops

See pages 10 and 11

Astronauts will orbit the kitchen to explore these pops.

Cocoa Peanut Planet Pops

● In a blender container combine ¾ cup *milk*, ½ cup *peanut butter*, ¼ cup *nonfat dry milk powder*, ¼ cup *plain yogurt*, 1 tablespoon *unsweetened cocoa powder*, and 2 tablespoons *honey*. Cover and blend till smooth.

● Pour the mixture into four 5-ounce paper cups. Cover with foil. Insert wooden sticks through the foil into mixture. Freeze overnight or till firm. To serve, remove foil and tear off cup. Makes 4.

Space Station

See pages 12 and 13

On page 13 Saturn is visible in the space station window. Tell your children a little about it.

● Saturn is a huge planet. It is much bigger than Earth.

● Saturn has beautiful rings that circle its middle. The rings are made of pieces of ice and rock. Some of the pieces are as small as dust and some are as big as a house.

Control Panel

See pages 14 and 15

After your children decorate the Control Panel, make a base for it with the lid of the shoe box. Here's how:

Turn the lid upside down. Set the bottom of the Control Panel in the lid. Prop the bottom edge of the Control Panel on the edge of the lid so the box is tilting back slightly. On the back, tape the Control Panel to the lid.

Shiny Robot

See pages 16 and 17

A box of any size or shape can work for the robot's body. For the big robot on the left side of the photo on page 17, we used a large oatmeal container. Here's what to do:

Cover the container with foil. For arms, cut a hole on each side of the container the size of a toilet paper tube. Push 1 tube through each hole. Cover the arms with foil. For the head, decorate a small box with a face. Glue or tape it to the top of the container.
● Reading suggestion: *Robot-Bot-Bot* by Fernando Krahn

Stars, Stars, Stars

See pages 18 and 19

While your children study the stars, they might like to nibble on these special cookies.

Twinkling Star Cookies

● In a large mixer bowl beat ⅓ cup *margarine or butter* and ⅓ cup *shortening* with an electric mixer on medium to high speed for 30 seconds. Add 1 cup *all-purpose flour* to the margarine. Then add 1 *egg*, ¾ cup *sugar*, 1 tablespoon *milk*, 1 teaspoon *baking powder*, 1 teaspoon *vanilla*, and a dash *salt*. Beat till thoroughly combined. Beat or stir in another 1 cup *all-purpose flour*. Divide dough in half. Cover and chill for 3 hours.
● On a lightly floured surface, roll *half* the dough to ⅛-inch thickness. Cut dough into star shapes. Place on a *foil-lined* cookie sheet. Cut out small star shapes in cookie centers. Spoon ½ cup finely crushed *hard candy* into cookie centers to fill holes.
● Bake in a 375° oven for 7 to 8 minutes or till edges are firm and bottoms are very lightly browned. Cool cookies on foil;

remove. Store in a covered container. (If desired, omit candy centers. Sprinkle the cookies with colored sugar before baking.) Makes 36 to 48.

Shooting Stars

See pages 20 and 21

Children will enjoy this painting project. In fact, they like creating all kinds of artwork.

When they share their work with you, ask them to tell you about their drawings. Avoid asking "What is it?" or commenting "What a pretty picture." Instead, try "I like these squiggly lines. How did you make them?" or "I like the colors you used." Specific comments about their work shows your interest and acknowledges their artistic process.

Space Scope

Young astronauts easily can make a pretend telescope.

● Push a *4-inch cardboard tube (toilet paper tube)* about halfway into 1 end of an *11-inch cardboard tube (paper towel tube)*. It should fit tightly enough so it doesn't slide through.
● On a 4-inch square of *waxed paper* use a *pencil* to trace around the end of the long tube, making a circle. Lay a few *star-shaped sequins* or *shiny confetti* inside the circle you drew on the waxed paper. Lay another 4-inch square of waxed paper on top of the first piece with the stars in between the papers.
● Take the end of the long tube and place it over the waxed paper circle with the stars inside. Wrap the ends of the waxed paper around the tube. Use a *rubber band* to hold the waxed paper on the tube. Hold the Space Scope up to your eye and turn the large cardboard tube. You'll see the stars move.

Jar of Stars

See pages 22 and 23

As your children watch the stars go by, discuss these vocabulary words about space.

Planet: A world that travels around the sun. Earth is the planet where we live.

Solar system: The sun and the objects that move around it, such as planets and moons.

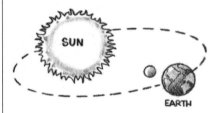

Galaxy: A huge family of stars that includes our solar system. Earth is in a galaxy called the Milky Way.

Orbit: The path objects follow in space.

Space Creatures' Spaceships

See pages 24 and 25

As you talk with your children about pretend space creatures, read this rhyme just for fun.

What do Spacelings look like?
And what do Spacelings do?
In my life I've not seen one.
In your whole life, have you?

I bet they're cute and friendly.
Of course, I have no clues.
But wouldn't it be something
If they looked like me and you?

● Reading suggestions:
Company's Coming
    by Arthur Yorinks
My Friend from Outer Space
    by Caroline Arnold

Flying Saucer

See pages 26 and 27

After exploring outer space through their imagination, your children might enjoy exploring outside your home.

While the sun is out, explain that it warms Earth and that flowers need the sun to grow. Have your children touch things like a rock and ask if they know why it's warm. In the evening, talk about the stars and planets.

During the exploration, encourage your children to discuss their observations. This is a fun way for them to learn about science.

Spaceship Sandwiches

See pages 28 and 29

Before your children start their sandwiches, you'll need to assemble these ingredients.

Filling Ingredients

    1 cup chopped cooked beef
    ½ cup shredded carrot
    1 3-ounce package cream
       cheese, cut into cubes
       and softened
    2 tablespoons sweet pickle
       relish
       Dash pepper

Spaceship Cake

Make a cake that's out of this world for your children's next party. You'll need:

● One 8- or 9-inch round baked cake layer
● 3 cups white frosting
● Food coloring (optional)
● Assorted candies and/or cookies.

Cut the cake following the first diagram below. First, cut a 2-inch slice from the cake. Then cut the slice in half.

Join the pieces together with some of the frosting, as shown in the second diagram below. If desired, use food coloring to tint some of the frosting. Frost the cake any way you like. Decorate the cake as desired with candies and/or cookies.

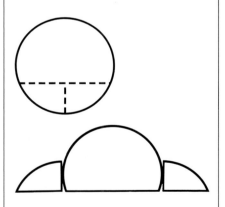

BETTER HOMES AND GARDENS® BOOKS

Editor: Gerald M. Knox   Art Director: Ernest Shelton   Managing Editor: David A. Kirchner
Family Life Editor: Sharyl Heiken

OUTER SPACE

Editors: Jennifer Darling and Sandra Granseth   Graphic Designers: Harjis Priekulis and Linda Vermie
Project Manager: Jennifer Speer Ramundt
Contributing Illustrator: Buck Jones   Contributing Photographer: Scott Little

Have BETTER HOMES AND GARDENS® magazine delivered to your door.
For information write to: ROBERT AUSTIN, P.O. BOX 4536, DES MOINES, IA 50336